Treasure Hunt

CHAPTERS

by Meish Goldish   illustrated by Lyle Miller

**Harcourt**

Orlando   Boston   Dallas   Chicago   San Diego

Visit *The Learning Site!*
www.harcourtschool.com

WHAT IS METAL?

You use it when you wear a watch. You use it when you open a can of soup. You use it when you put a quarter into a pay phone.

What do you use? Metal!

Metal is usually hard and shiny. Iron, gold, and silver are metals. So are nickel, lead, zinc, copper, aluminum, and tin. Steel is a metal that is made from iron and other materials.

Many things are made of metal. That's because metal can be melted and formed into many shapes. The shapes can be large or small, sturdy or delicate.

Look around the room. Do you see a paper clip? A lamp? A key? Those things are often made of metal or have metal parts.

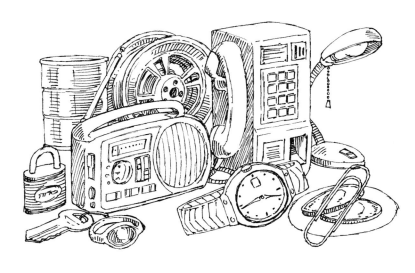

penny **nickel** **dime** **quarter**

half-dollar **dollar**

The coins we use for money are made of metal.
However, each coin is a mix of different metals.

A penny is mostly zinc with a coating of copper.
The copper gives the coin its brown color.

A nickel is a mix of nickel and copper.

A dime, a quarter, a half-dollar, and a dollar also
are mixes of nickel and copper. These four coins all
have three layers. The middle layer is copper. The
two outside layers are a mix of nickel and copper.

Think about the different metals in coins the
next time you are counting your money.

Metal comes from the earth. There is a lot of metal deep in the earth. If you could dig ten miles down, you'd find aluminum and iron.

If you could dig even deeper, you'd find more metals. Many scientists think the center of the earth is made of nickel and iron.

You may have read about workers who dig in the earth to find metal. Some of them search for profitable metals such as gold, silver, or copper. These rugged workers are called miners. When miners find the metal they are searching for, they dig it out of the earth. Then the metal is used to make jewelry, tools, and other things.

Thousands of years ago, people began digging in the earth for tin and copper. They mixed those two metals to make bronze. They made tools out of bronze. They also found iron in the earth and used it to make tools and weapons.

Gold and silver might be called multicultural metals. They appeal to people all over the world. These metals are used to make jewelry, statues, plates, goblets, and other objects.

People decorate themselves and their homes with metal objects of many kinds. Since metal lasts a long time, they can pass valuable metal objects on to their children.

Mining began in the United States almost 300 years ago. Back then, the French mined zinc and lead along the Mississippi River.

In 1848, a miner found gold in the hills of California. Because gold is difficult to find and beautiful, it is valuable. People especially like jewelry made of gold. This metal almost beckons people to touch it.

The news of finding gold in California quickly spread around the world. However, people could not simply pay air fares and fly to California. They had to travel by horseback and covered wagon. By 1849, thousands of people had rushed to California. They hoped to find some of that gold and get rich.

The hopeful California miners looked for gold the hard way. Most of them simply scooped up small rocks and put them in a tin pan. Then they rinsed off the dirt, hoping to spot small chunks of gleaming gold. Their work was called "panning."

The miners panned all day long. It was a very tiring job. Most days they didn't find any gold. Often they would find "fool's gold." Fool's gold looks like gold, but it is a common metal called pyrite. Real gold melts when heated. Fool's gold smokes and smells bad.

The California gold rush led to more gold hunts in the United States. Many gold mines were set up in the West and the South. In time, however, most of the gold was mined, and the mines were abandoned. Still, miners did find other valuable metals, including copper, lead, and silver.

Today, people still hunt for gold and other metals. Now it's easier because they can use metal detectors.

WHAT IS A METAL DETECTOR?

A metal detector is a machine that finds metal. It is like a hunting dog—but it doesn't bark!

Metal might be hidden or lost in the grass. It could be buried in the sand or soil. It may even be behind a brick or stone wall. If metal is nearby, the metal detector will find it.

Suppose you lost a silver ring or coin. You might think your ring or coin was gone forever. Don't worry! You can use a metal detector to find it.

Metal detectors are very accurate. Some can even tell you if the metal you found is worth a lot of money.

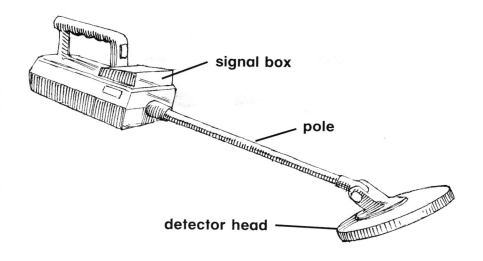

signal box

pole

detector head

Metal detectors come in different shapes and sizes. They are used for different jobs.

People who hunt for coins or gold use one kind of detector. It is a long pole with a round plate connected to the end. The plate is called a *detector head*. The other end of the pole is connected to a *signal box*.

To find metal, you hold the detector head close to the ground. By walking slowly around an area, you can discover if metal is nearby.

The signal box on the pole is important. It lets the user know if metal is in the area.

Not all signal boxes are the same. Some have an arrow inside. If metal is nearby, the arrow points toward it.

Other signal boxes have a light. If metal is near, the light goes on.

Still other signal boxes have a speaker. If metal is near, the speaker makes noise. The noise gets louder as the detector gets closer to the metal.

Metal detectors also have different strengths. A low-power detector can find metal up to 2 feet away. A high-power detector can find metal that is farther away.

HOW DOES A METAL DETECTOR WORK?

A metal detector sends out a signal. Objects with no metal in them do not respond to the signal. However, a metal object sends a signal back to the detector. It's as if the detector and the metal are talking to each other.

Then the metal detector sends a signal to the person holding it, using an arrow, light, or noise. It tells him or her that metal is nearby. The diagram on the next page shows how a metal detector finds a coin in the ground. Look at the diagram as you read the steps.

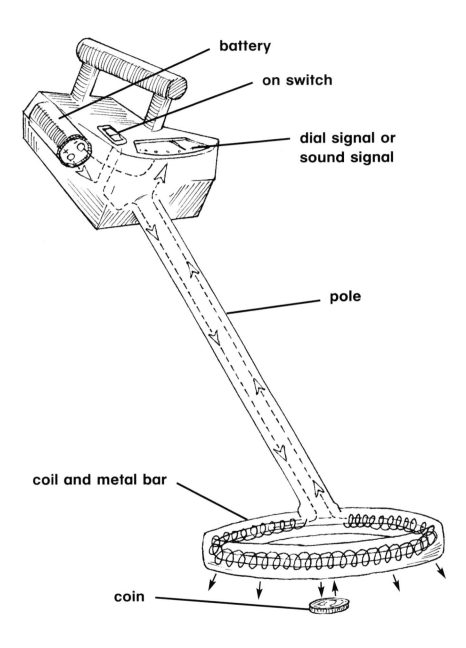

battery

on switch

dial signal or
sound signal

pole

coil and metal bar

coin

12

1   The hunt begins when the person turns on the detector. Electricity flows through a coil in the detector head.

2   The coil is wrapped around a metal bar. The electricity turns the bar into a magnet.

3   The bar creates a magnetic field. This area around a magnet has the power to attract metal.

4   The magnetic field travels into the ground. It reaches the metal coin.

5   Energy from the magnetic field makes electricity flow through the coin. Now both the bar and the coin are magnets.

6   Energy from the coin's magnetic field travels back to the coil.

7   Electricity flows to the signal box. The box indicates that metal has been found.

Today, many people use metal detectors. Some use them for work, and others use them for fun.

Engineers use metal detectors to find pipelines in the ground. That saves them from digging up a whole area to find the line. It also prevents accidentally digging into the line and breaking the pipe!

Scientists also use metal detectors. Some kinds of scientists use the detectors to find and identify metals that are a natural part of the earth. Different kinds of scientists use detectors to locate old tools, coins, and other objects that ancient people left behind. These objects tell the scientists about the people who used to live there.

Other workers use metal detectors in different ways. Airport workers ask passengers to walk through a metal detector before they get on an airplane. The detector checks for metal in their pockets and bags.

Traffic engineers use metal detectors to count the cars that drive down a street. Detectors also send signals to change the traffic lights.

You may have used a metal detector without knowing it. Did you ever buy a snack from a vending machine? A metal detector inside knows the kind and amount of metal in each coin. That way, the machine knows which coin you inserted. Then it can give you the correct change!

Metal detectors aren't just for work. Many people use them for fun. They will tell you that metal detecting is relaxing.

Today, treasure hunts are a popular hobby. People use metal detectors to hunt for old coins, rings, and other objects. What they find can be worth a lot of money.

Some hunters look in parks, and others go to beaches. Like the California miners, some people still head for the hills. They use metal detectors in hopes of finding gold.

If you get a chance, try out a metal detector. Who knows what you may find on your treasure hunt!